Toddler

COLORING

BOOK

Numbers colors shapes

Toddler
COLORING BOOK
Numbers colors shapes

This book belongs to:

Name _ _ _ _ _ _ _ _ _ _ _ _ _ _ _ _

Age _ _ _ _ _ _ _ _ _ _

Numbers

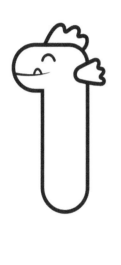  

ZERO

ONE

TWO

THREE

FOUR

FIVE

SIX

SEVEN

EIGHT

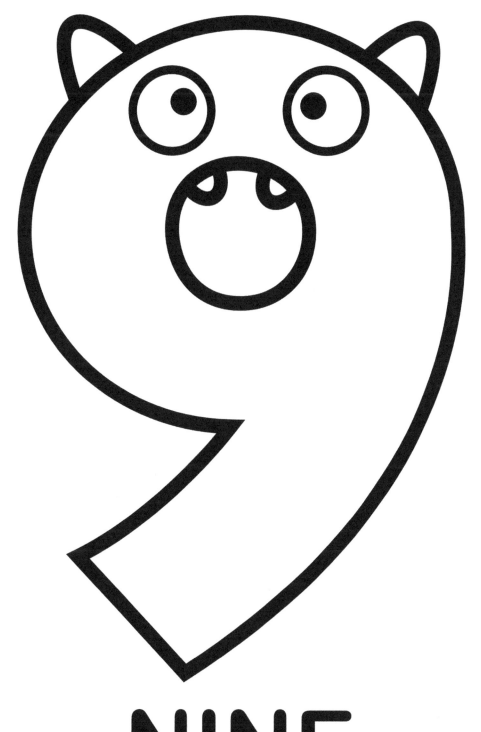

NINE

TEN

ELEVEN

TWELVE

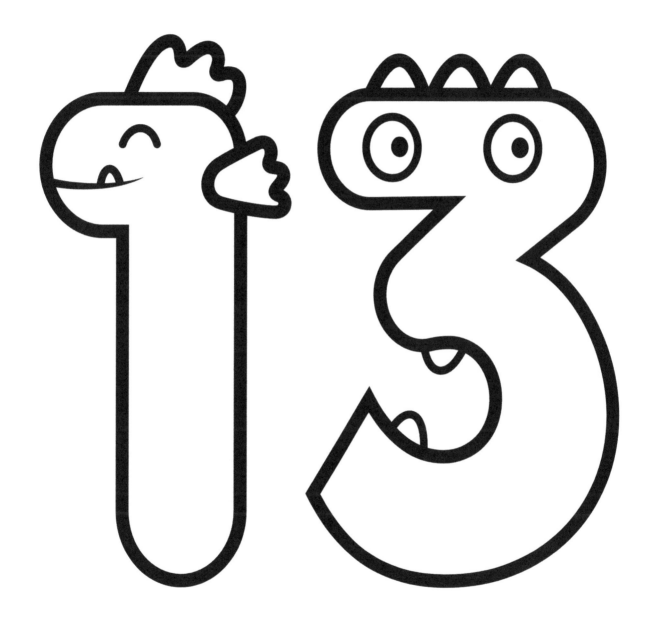

THIRTEEN

FOURTEEN

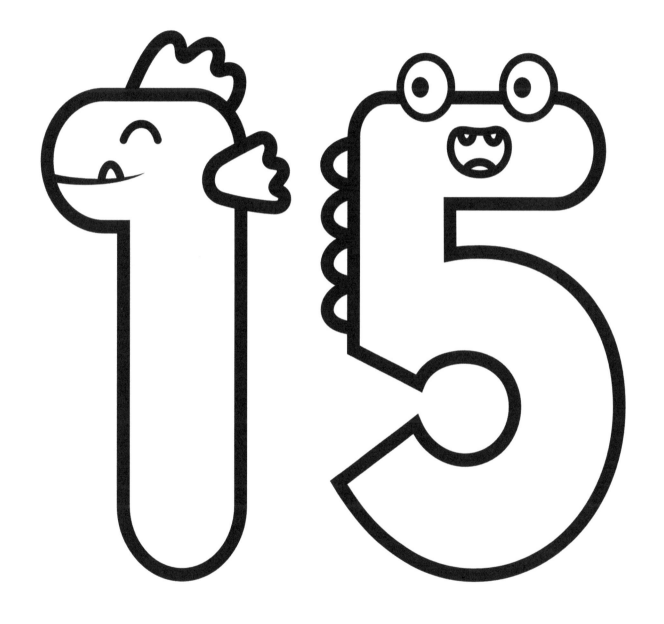

FIFTEEN

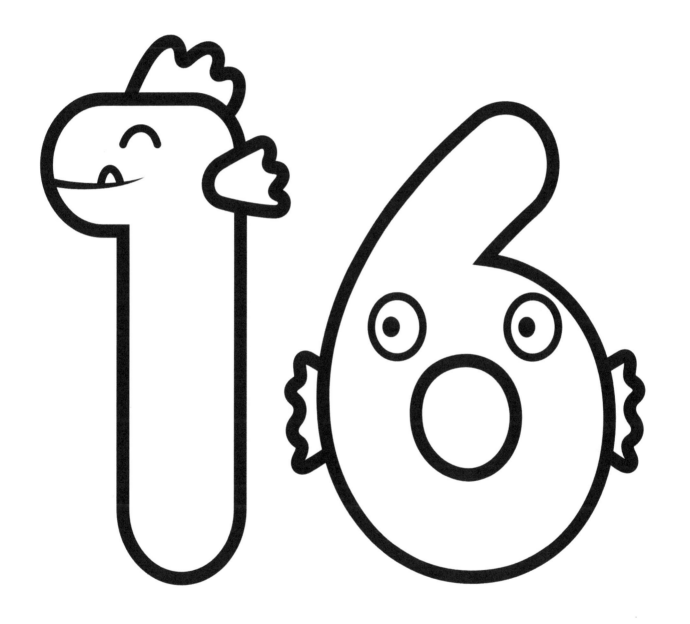

SIXTEEN

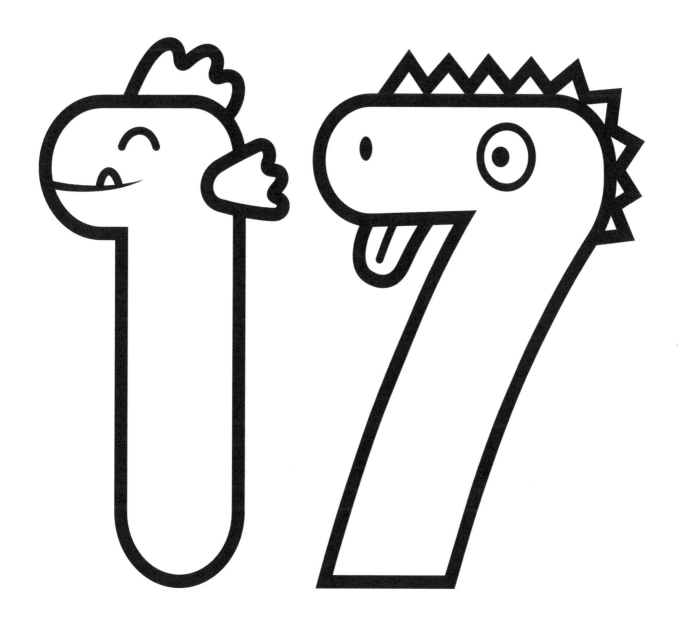

SEVENTEEN

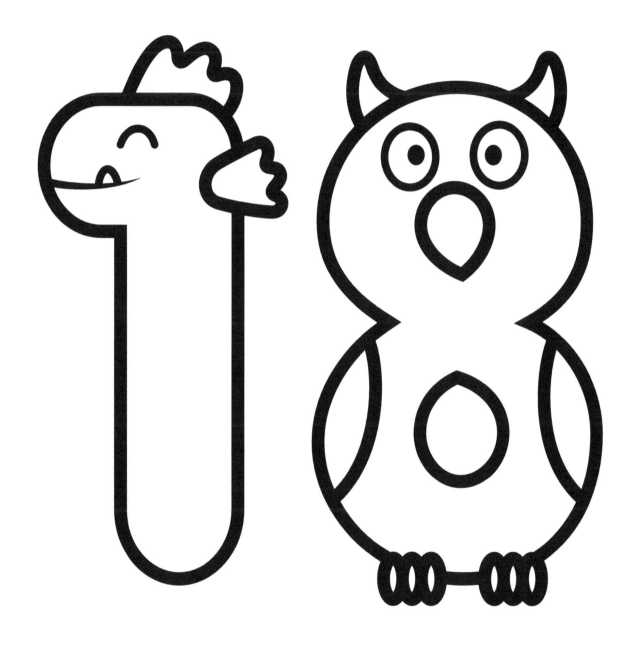

EIGHTEEN

NINETEEN

TWENTY

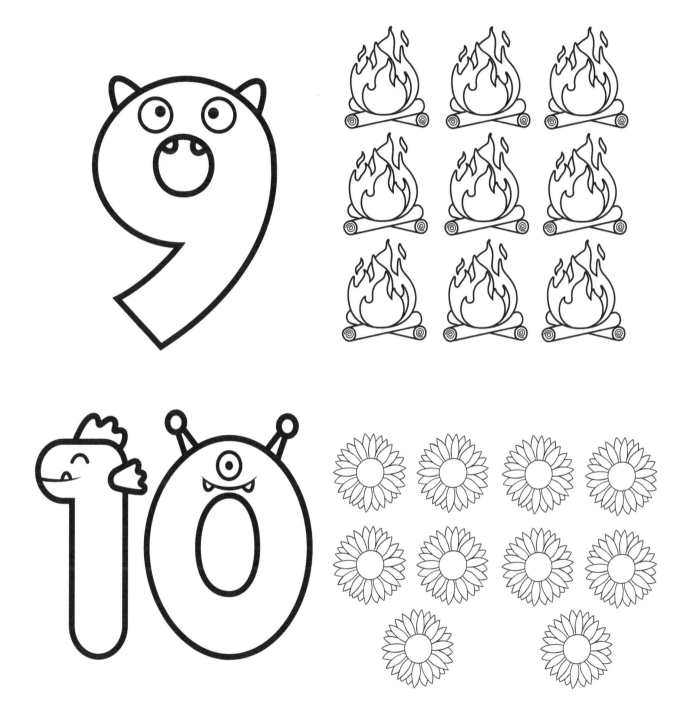

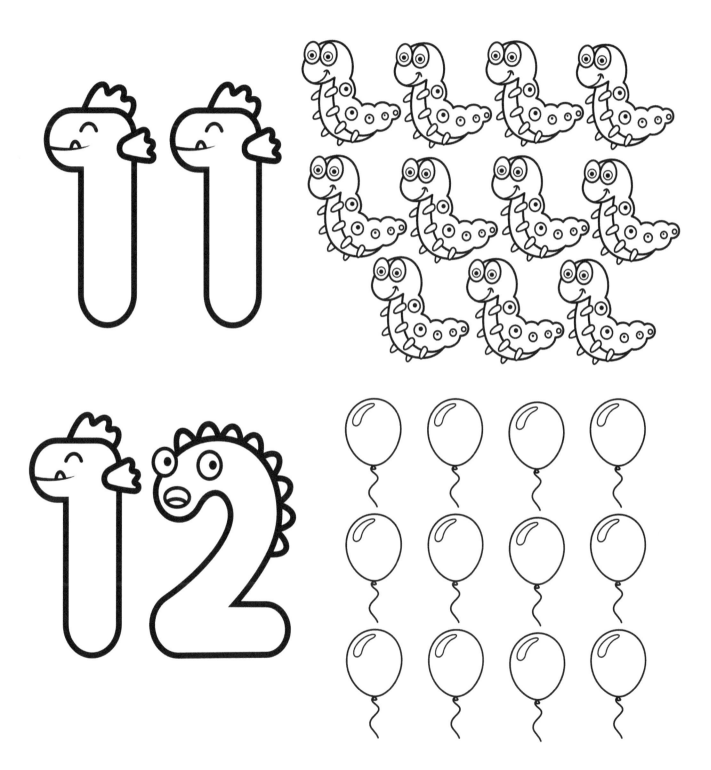

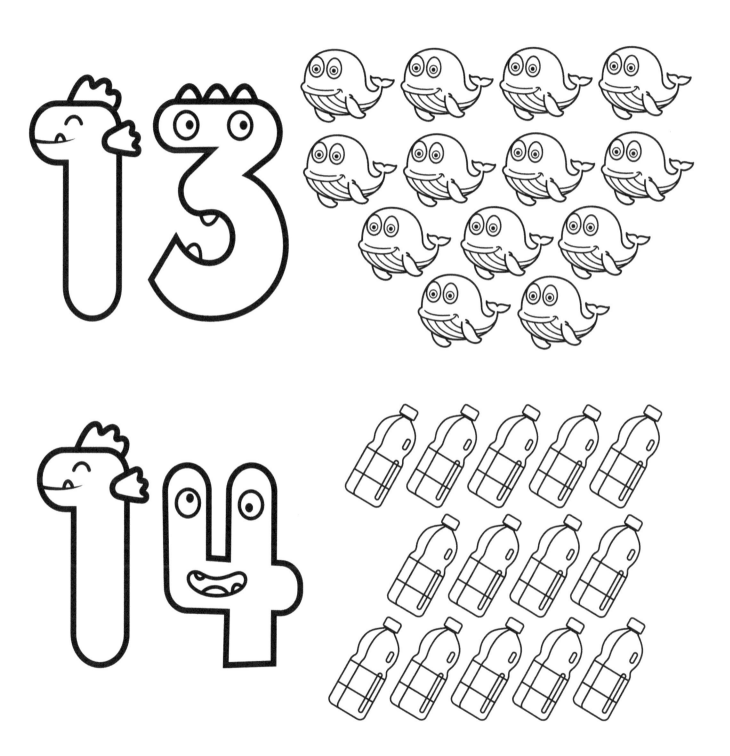

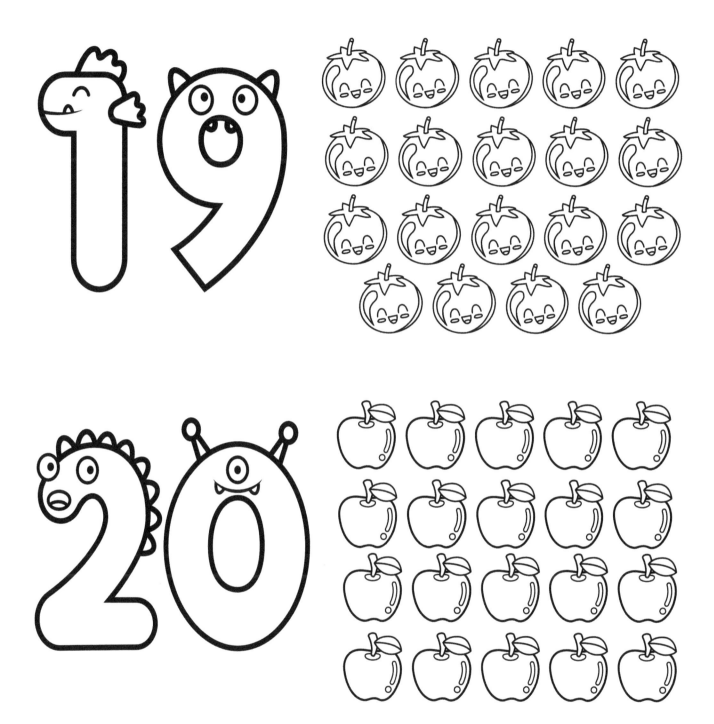

Colors

Red

Orange

Yellow

Pink

Purple

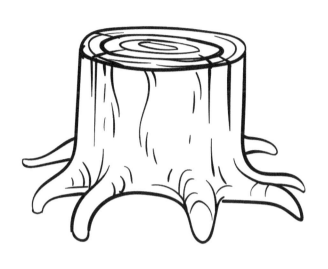

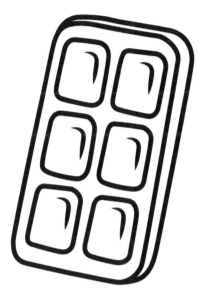

Brown

Green

Blue

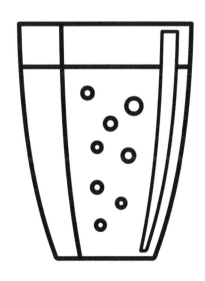

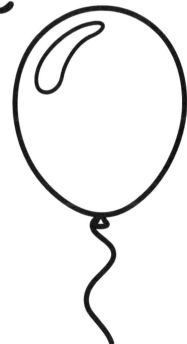

Red

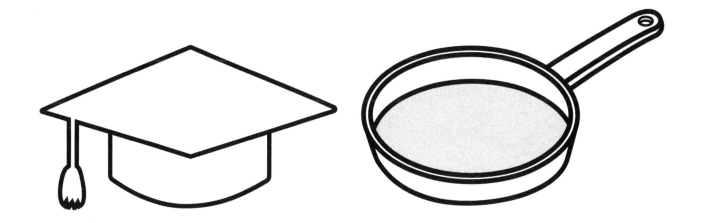

Black

Shapes

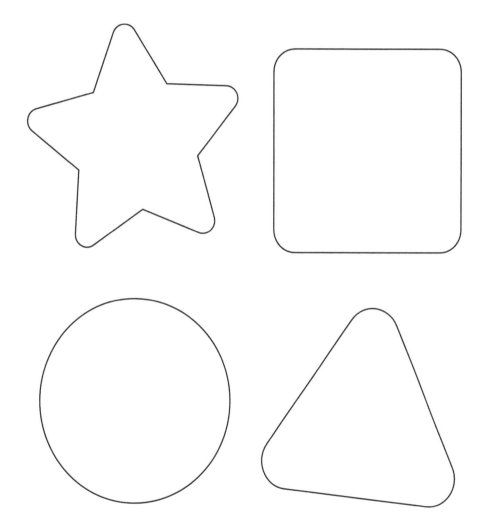

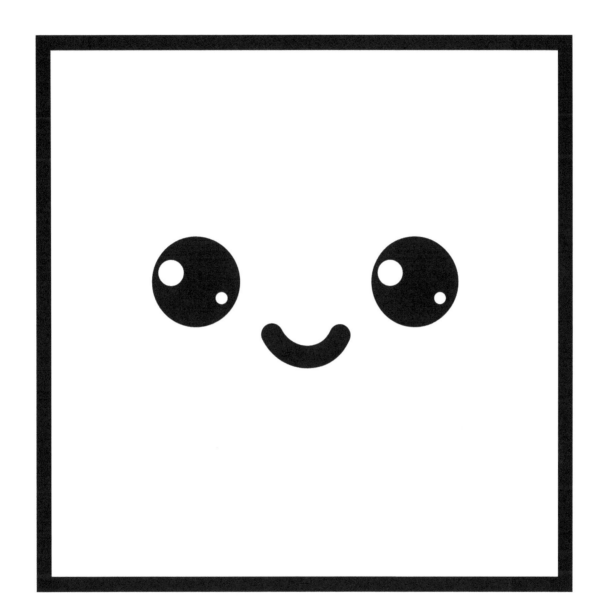

SQUARE

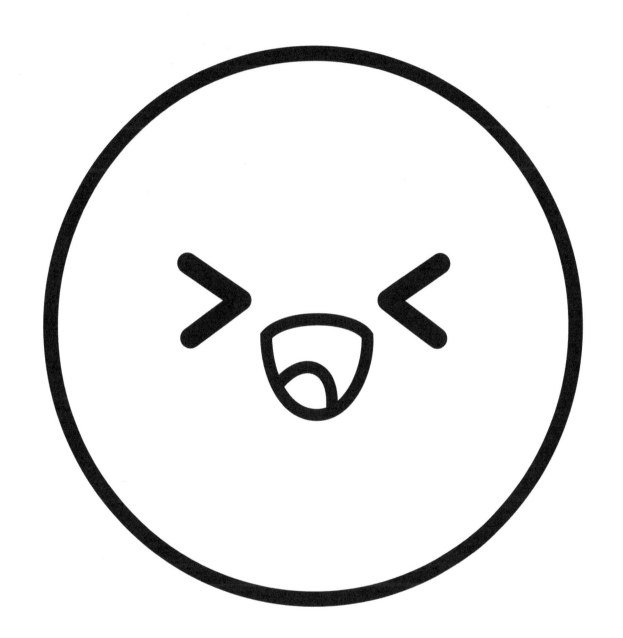

CIRCLE

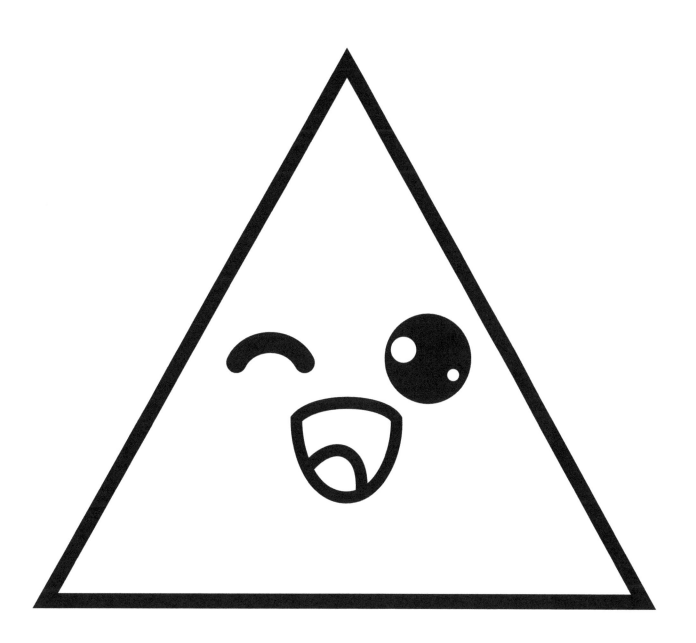

TRIANGLE

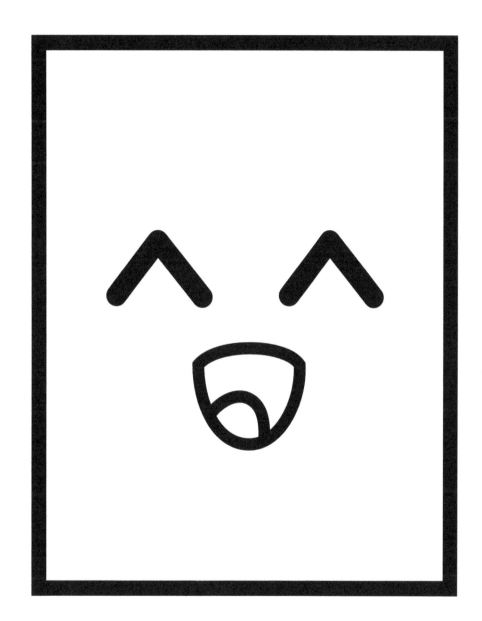

RECTANGLE

OVAL

HEART

STAR

DIAMOND

CPSIA information can be obtained
at www.ICGtesting.com
Printed in the USA
LVHW062154200323
742124LV00014B/829